YOU ARE HERE

You Are Here

Cover art: 'Overview ' © David Dewis 2006
Heaventree logo design by Panna Chauhan

Published in the UK by
The Heaventree Press,
Koco Building, The Arches,
Spon End, Coventry CV1 3JQ

Printed in the UK by
Cromwell Press, Trowbridge, Wiltshire BA14 0XB

We are grateful for the financial support of ARTS COUNCIL ENGLAND

YOU ARE HERE

Simon Turner

The Heaventree Press

ACKNOWLEDGEMENTS

Some of these poems have previously appeared in *Avocado* ('The Magic Hour' and 'Geographies'), *Liminal Pleasures* ('Joseph Stella's Reality Frenzy', 'Dada Jukebox') and *Intercapillary Space* ('To Be Bewildered' and section two of 'La Città Nuova').

'Earthworks' was originally written as a commission for the Herbert Art Gallery in Coventry.

CONTENTS

IV Municipal Amenities   **75**

Logos: Two German Poems

I: Friedrich von Logau, 'Der Buchstabe tötet'

Letter, you're a killer,
a cuntish gouge
in the page's white earth

Whoever's feart
of the gaped gravemouth
had best keep back
from the black lip
of you & yourn

No wonder folk these days
have left off from
squinnying & scribbling
your alphabet's scotched woods

II: Gottfried Benn, 'Ein Wort, ein Satz'

The word, breeding a sentence:
life, a plain sense of it,
stutters out of language—
the sun canters to a halt,
planets clam up & the word
drags the whole shebang
into its orbit

The word—a gash of light
a Boeing scooching off the runway
a humped pyre with a scarf of flame
a shooting star

& now the dark again,
bulky & terrible, charging into the vacuum
bunched around the earth & me

I

Groundwork

Purple Toadflax

Thriving amid trashed stone,
an imperious purple spear
thrusts up through mizzling rain,
tough roots nudging under rubble;

a promiscuous weed, flaunting itself
speechlessly until we unearthed
its given name tucked inside
a guide to British wildflowers—

purple toadflax—then emerging
from the stacked wreckage
of the unnamed, the unnameable,
into fiery coherence on the page.

Something for a Fisher

A scuffed place, this:
the pond, lugging at its edges
frothed algae and the season's last
or first dropped leaves, slops
against the moistened bank
where fishers hoist their lines
at diagonals in trim light.

They'll bring nothing home,
nothing to surface—the carp gawping
behind swirled curtains of silt
decline the bait—unless the sight
of a moorhen strutting on
spindleshanks across the bank
is a catch, or turned earth's stink
under the stripped trees.

Even so, they'll not start back
until last light, traipsing up the rise
to bring the sun into view; past
ramshackle alders that draw apart
to bracket and perfect for one
stuck beat the high rise estates,
glaucous, hunched, remote,
their halt geometry a stuttered plea
the crazed sky ponders and declines.

Storm Journal: *23rd July 2006*

Watching the storm from the bathroom window,
rain-blasts gusting in, and the holly
shaking its leaves with every batter of water.
I thought, "The tough green tongues quake
in their multiples," but it was nonsense.
I discarded it. Yet they did quake, the leaves,
shuddering with every plosive shrapnel-scrap of rain
that hammered down, with every shiver of the shifting wind
they shook, flinging silver fistfuls of rain
to the ground. The windows rattled with the thunder,
great booming cadenzas of it rolling down,
distant thunder, lightning blaring from the thunderheads
in clutches of twos and threes, some of it far off,
skimming the cloud's height, some near enough
to flummox the air with the sound of tearing fabric.

Earthworks

I

Storm wreckage on the Sarehole river walk,
willows horizontalled and huddled down
on the floodplain, in the flattened sedge,
clutching tough mats of moss and clay
in their gnarled, flourished root-fists:
a clutter of compass points, the earth's splayed map.

II

Hel Tor, cleft rock,
cloud shadows racing
over oceans of rape.

There's rain to the east,
backlit thunderheads
clambering godwards

and me atop this stone skull
watching two sea-blown shrimp
writhe and curl in a pool

of the morning's rain.
It is a universe to them.
They are provided for.

III

Bleached ash stumps have punched
through the cobbled rise that slopes
up towards the A road overpass
spanning the Dunkirk canal, each one
brandishing its bunch of spring leaves:
the first wave.

The Weir

1

where the river shows
its rage by tumbling
down level after
level of stone &
enacts in miniature
its own fuming
descent from rock-
spring to sea-mouth
then climaxing
its falling in leaping
tendrils of froth
before slackening
its tensed currents
to become a black
stillness is where
four crows flew in
to rest on a jut
of jumbled rock
one of them strutting
to the water's
calmed edge to clean
its glossy wings off

2

the tree-trunk snagged
lengthways at the weir's top

a caesura
        an elision

not to be budged by the force
tonne after tonne of motive water

at bottom
     a brittle black
branch
   emerging
     from white
spray   its
      off-cut

Fall

One of the three primary branches
of next door's lilac tree
has snapped & fallen
against the wall, its tough
polished leaves concealing
neat stacks of leftover bricks

White wood glares
through the split bark;
browned leaves & clusters of
shrivelled flowers depend
from the still-upright primaries—

the hobbled branch
is most alive

Buddleia

Named by or for some
dead famous Adam its
flourished prongs are
aggregates of minute

purple flowers, furled
petals pursed round pollen-
soaked hubs, the upper-
most of each tapered

clutch effervescent,
those clustered hugger-
mugger at the base shrunk
to brittle, starveling, dis-

regardable dreck—

Storm Journal: *26ᵗʰ July 2006*

1.

Dry thunder, neon flashes
on the house fronts, the broad fir
humped like a fortress of night,
its immensity, its stillness.

Dry thunder, not a glim of rain.
The sky's a gauzy indigo, smirring
into violet nearer to the skyline,
rooftops and tree-shapes straggle-ragged.
The storm doesn't yet know what it is;
it steps gently out of the south,
straddles the river.

                          Dry thunder,
distant thunder, coming no closer.

2.

Night-walk. Stink of roads, baked through the day,
tin-smatter of rain, rust-blotches on the paving,
dry beneath the beech where the downpour
yammers its gamelan through blood-dark leaves.
Bubbles coast streams to the guttering,
grass patches parched to straw, greedy
for the deluge. Trees, chameleoned against the night,
chuck chiaroscuro blots with every photoflare.

Back home, soaked through, we watch the storm
bawl its *Rastì Roustì* over the garden, the alleyway,
the further houses. The lightning's fire-strikes
just out of shot, the thunder growling, deep-end register,
and the earth giving off that clean wet smell, sopped
right down to the under-rock, coming alive,
every leaf flashing in its dustless gloss.
The neighbour's England flags are drenched
to dishcloths, limpet-clinging to their hanging-poles.
'Dark Side of the Moon' spills from the top floor window
of a tall house beyond the holly, beyond the clustered pines.

Moseley Bog

I

Dug pits here once
to plant young trees,
landslides of stones
and shale shaken loose
by blunt shovel blades
hacking the ground,
saplings' roots rammed home
into muck to punch
through rock and tap
the earth's bogged hoard—
snowmelt from March;
cracked crusts of winter's
frost-pools thawed and sunk;
autumn rain's seeped mulch
swaddled in the murk—
to feed, to leaf,
to breathe and persist.

II

It throngs, thrives, vaulting the stile,
scribbled loops and spillages of nettles and ivy
and wild garlic in frothy clutches thrusting beyond the margins
into Swanshurst's secluded yards,
where aerials tilt toothed beaks
to guzzle airborne static and the crows
blurt out Morse codes of alarm
from slant roofs and taut wire fences.

Light flares in latched windows,
behind the bog's crests of beech—
lead flickers to gold in the first case;
in the second, a blackened mass
crowned with white fire blooms and concludes.

The Dingles

A named site,
a provided set
of conditions
& relations—

pigeon lofts with peeling slivers
of last century's paint
crackling & dropping off
their bungled planks,
structures flustered with feathered
*ooo*s & *aaa*s: a thralled audience

a splayed willow
bending to still water,
mirrored gloss where
its yellow leaves
are held & petrified,
clapped in ice; a gallery
of its excellence

a tangled wad of trash
—tarpaulin, twine & wood—
smashing a massive capital **K**
up through the Cole's rush & push,
forcing its sibilance to break apart
& contend with this hard kick
to the throat then reconvene
its chastised currents & quicken

the water rat plunged
in the brisk river
that's big & spongy with spring,
pushing its body forwards
through small labile waves,
forwards with pulsing strokes,
forwards to the bank
& up & out & forwards

swallows, towards dusk,
dotting the air like negative stars,
trim black shapes winking & dipping
over rooftops, over sycamore
& chestnut aligned & clarified
by the afternoon's dying filament,
a charged light glaring hard
before the bulb's blown & it's night—

a mute scaffold words
settle on: jays littering
blackened branches
smattered with rain
to bawl their noughts.

Sarehole

These black squealing tatters
are the bluing dusk becoming
a squall of birds and shaking clear
of the mill, hunched and shut;

clear and through, over stalled water,
tush of tall feathery grass,
to the town's frayed outskirts,
the farthest edges of speech.

Geographies

I:

Savage Nuneaton
munters in glottal-stopped rain

Juggernauts on the flyover
shunt & growl

In the backyard
two clothes pegs
turn tricks on the slumped line,
                    in a high wind

Storm-drains choke on guttural floods;
leaf debris & frothed bilge
gush from gobs of overflow pipes

Blown slates cluck tongues
on teeth as they shatter
fricative on tarmac

What umlauts for vowels do—
darken & thicken—
this storm enacts:
semis & towerblocks imbued
with the gravitas of Gothic script

II:

Why write? These things
are so much themselves—

industrial chimneys
with their five o'clock
shadows of soot, blushing
peach at dusk,
balking at the symbolism;

the gasworks, a brawny
contusion of light
& rust against the perfect
enamel of spring sky
appearing there, here,
in the gaps between
jagged back-to-backs
& shivered privet;

spiky-headed wildflowers
that jut & swagger
on the footpath, scent
of freshly rollocked turf—

that

III: The Fire Next Time

Spring runoff from the Pennines
enrages the river, churns the weir
to beer-froth. Submerged ash
& willow flail malnourished limbs;
drenched reeds stoop to ancient gods.

Marshland encroaches on the towpath:
schooners & barges bear the flood's brunt,
huddle at the quayside, kissing brick,
& glimpsed beneath the bridge's rickety planks,
a white surge of water, clenched, unleashed.

At the river's edge, boathouses & trashed shacks,
hoary & bluff as Old English syllables,
eye the wreckage & do not judge. Further out
a village church gestures with its gnarled spire
at the scorched parchment sky where three crows glide,
scrying their new alphabet.

IV: Blackgang

An ashy dark drawls down
onto the Chine, the stars
raked embers flaring up

Waves lisp under the cliffs,
lapping at loose-packed rock:
another inch this year—
sandstone, chalk, wrenched roots
of warped, edge-dwelling trees

Soon, the last houses nudging
the cliff's lip like chipped
& jaundiced teeth
will rot & topple
into the tongue-tied sea—

so, too, the condemned man's
last words drop
through silence

Storm Journal: *27ᵗʰ July 2006*

Storm comes in the guise of morning.
The sky's bleared chalk, light rain crescendos
to a drum-topple, an earth-flooding gush.
Lightning glitters, distant in the earliest moments,
soft trickles of thunder; later, brute strikes rucking
overhead, one punching down behind the houses opposite,
the air shredding itself, the sky whitewashed in light.
It's the thunder of skyscrapers tottering, struts
groaning to give up the ghost, or of galaxies forming
over billions of years, god-killing star-blossom.
The heart judders into life, the stalled blood
quickens and churns. Rain easing off now,
the thunder quelled, cadence of surf-crash, the lightning
no longer visible. Shreds of blue poke through
the thick-bundled cloud-crust, crows returning, landing
on rooftops to bark down the chimneypots,
testing their husky throats. Commuter traffic,
clatter of shovel-blade scraping on concrete.
Rain-pearls on the window-glass getting the light.

Bat-watching : summer : second night

Watts says of Zen:

"the world is seen as an inseparably interrelated field or
continuum, no part of which can actually be separated from the
rest or valued above or below the rest"

The garden's never still;
something's always breathing or
growing or kicking up a fuss
in the undergrowth—

                                pigeons
hacking at the bird cherry; the hedgehog
shuffling across the lawn to feed
and drink from the bowl on the top step

(first night, Dad sd "no bats this time" then
two of them mothing in from the east
whirled around the tree, the tree
                    a vertical darkness;
third night, too much wine, the foxgloves
upright and shameless, their frilled lips
gulping at the cooling air; fourth night,
blurts of rain and thunder, a single bat,
and the moon a sickle of apricot)

Swifts out in the failing light,
they're debugging the airwaves,
you phone, it's late, then
back outside, bats scarcely visible
scraps of the deepening indigo

Hui-neng "fundamentally, not
                 one thing exists"

The darkness spreads, and the bats,
the bats jink back to the trees, they've gone,
they've gone home to roost, and a passenger jet,
a passenger jet blinks its landing lights,
it's pushing through the humped clouds of
dusk, and the night's first star's pulsing
high above it, billions of years ago—

(29-6-2006 – 15-7-2006)

II

Book City

Bibliogenesis

In the beginning was the word
In the beginning was the worsted
In the beginning was the wraith
In the beginning was the wreck
In the beginning was the wrick
In the beginning was the writer
In the beginning was the wych-elm
In the beginning was the Xhosa
In the beginning was the yabber
In the beginning was the Yakut
In the beginning was the yank
In the beginning was the yarmulka
In the beginning was the yawn
In the beginning was the yell
In the beginning was the yersinia
In the beginning was the Yiddish
In the beginning was the ylang-ylang
In the beginning was the yokel
In the beginning was the Yorkie
In the beginning was the yo-yo

This is the book of the generations of Adam who begat Eve who begat Eruption who begat Volcano who begat Iceberg who begat Gobbledegook who begat Nonsense who begat Significance who begat Entropy who begat Death who begat Birth who begat Hacksaw who begat Hawk who begat Weasel who begat Liposuction who begat California who begat New York who begat Kittens who begat Milk who begat Charcoal who begat Limit who begat Edge who begat Centre who begat Elemental who begat Primitive who begat Futuristic who begat Candy who begat Cotton who begat Vinyl who begat Lumberjack who begat Canada who begat Mexico who begat Orgasm who begat Pleasure who begat Pain who begat Narwhal who begat Unicorn who begat Crow who begat Wobble who begat Shake who begat Steady who begat Yesterday who begat Today who begat Tomorrow who begat Worm who begat Tequila who begat Jesus who begat Summer who begat Swallow who begat Spit who begat Thunder who begat Rain who begat Sahara who begat Adam who

& Astrogoth said "Let there be lhasa apsos"
& Bobbi-Bobbi said "Let there be libel"
& Chukwa said "Let there be Libra"
& Dionysus said "Let there be lichen"
& Erlik said "Let there be lidocaine"
& Freya said "Let there be lieutenants"
& God said "Let there be light"
& Hermes said "Let there be Lilliputians"
& Ifejioku said "Let there be limbo"
& Janus said "Let there be limnologists"
& Ka said "Let there be limpidity"
& Loki said "Let there be lindens"
& Marduk said "Let there be lingo"
& Nephthys said "Let there be linnets"
& Osiris said "Let there be lint"
& Pan-gu said "Let there be liquescence"
& Quetzlcoatl said "Let there be lisping"
& Ra said "Let there be literalism"
& Shiva said "Let there be Lithia"
& Tiamat said "Let there be Lithuanians"
& Uthlanga said "Let there be little"
& Vishnu said "Let there be liver"
& Wodin said "Let there be llamas"
& Xochiquetzal said "Let there be loathing"
& Yarilo said "Let there be lobotomies"
& Zeus said "Let there be lochia"

"the poem is nothing"

i

the poem is nothing
if not an anvil

scolding spikes of tangerine get
hammered into various shapes on its surface

maybe a wild black horse or
a scrap of the moon or a girl
sitting on the rim of a fountain
about to fall in or not
about to fall in & ruin her good summer dress
or a set of steel teeth with a winding mechanism
big enough to chew the entire city up
munch munch off it goes

glaring sparks rainbow through the air
they could start fires but the poem
stays cool black motionless & there
you can't shift it now

ii

the poem is nothing if not an anvil
it whistles down the coyote gets it

Thirteen

I

sing 'snow' on a wet
night not 'love'
this beaked red 'what if'

II

moth swims reef din
kite are
here in the barbed lake switch

III

dam builder thud this wind table when brick
maps fat sail in a rope the wall

IV

now mad man
near one
black bandanna android maw
neo-ear

V

horrified thorn kow-tow
in the fealty of bones
the nouns feed on yet
ignited ash
                fur rose

VI

loco finches wing wide till
air barbs clash twigs
the shock of a ribbed thaw
a dross of tied corn
          mote
heart on **'dead'** switch
hide cause in parable

VII

a mad tide moon
his bold round image wind
on slick water the buoyed
heart's *auto da fé*
tow the name of you

VIII

blent ikon a snow
scratches a blind day lupine
ubu town kit
divide a slant block birth the
thin ikon

IX

white hubstone lightfucked raw
mirthdead
nonescream offcoil

X

a cleft ghost this dark
failing grey night
weave the spun bone
clash loudly troy

XI

cover the rude connect
slang chains
chafe me oread pincer
he took a thin mist
how quiet pages of his head
cold firs bark

XII

tv movie ring hire
beastly finger mulch

XIII

gentle waves root in a nail
now is 'ing'
& was is not 'ing'
a red silk bath
clears the mind

Autumn Processional

September survives but transmitted.

Holding account of the outbreaks of clarity.

Summer & the limit of maximum.

Of straight blue, the yellow aspect.

Tremble egg, because complete.

Time crisping, or inserted into light.

Simple branches in the new black holes.

Cones reciprocated the trees, which support crystals.

A yellow trembling.

What is the latter? Hardly salt.

Purposes of the cloud.

If only the tree were considered.

On a long-term basis to tremble the yellow sheets.

Another dish developed.

Destroyed again construct.

An inclination in the leaves.

Examined branches.

Cut-out cover rebuilt by existence.

It shakes with the blackness.

Behind capacities, fine clouds.

Existence: the reconstructed school.

It has exchanged the trees.

Another developed plate of constructions.

The tremble survives, however she's transferred it.

The last one is not bad.

Dada Jukebox
chart rundown jam for and after Peter Finch

Nova Posse, "Slightly Kinky, Slightly Japanese"
BJ Mapplethorpe & the Hoodoo Scribblers, "Cincinnati Tailspin"
The Detroit Hammers, "Live at Innsbruck"
Squawkbox Manifest, "Trombone Slaughterhouse"
Cassandra Slumgulleon, "Nature Shows No Mercy"
'Moses' Fellaheen & the Collapsible Toes, "Big by Big"
The Sonny Pynchon Horn Ensemble, "Heavy Bop"
Vosht, "The Balloon of Perhaps"
Hector Mac Low, "Concerto for Treated Dulcimer and Cardboard Banjo"
My Name is Peter, "My Name is Peter"
The Crates, "Applicability is Now!"
Lightning Hellespont, "Downriver Fingerpie Blues"
Spleen, "We Rock, You Suck"
Popply Nogood & the Phantom Band, "And What Will Become of Them?"

To Be Bewildered

I wrote this piece for John Cage;
it has something to do with John Cage:
John Cage caught in a traffic jam;
John Cage and his mother;
Cage on the East Coast
sipping iced tea with John Cage.
Cage is going round universities,
although Cage admits a multiplicity.
What about the Cage influence?
Well, I mean, Cage was great;
I respect Cage and I got to know him a little:
I've always respected Cage.
Many of us have a debt to Cage:
everybody has read John Cage's writings;
this book began with John Cage.
Look at the way Cage worked,
writing music that sounds like Cage,
five minutes in length and open, like Cage:
of course, that's what Cage was very good at.
What you like in John Cage is John Cage,
although Cage would never say it like that:
un-Cage-like.
I had the chance of actually seeing Cage—
by following what Cage said
I went down to Cage's to use his piano:
Cage's comment inspired the experiment.
The philosophies of John Cage—
John Cage's music, for instance;
John Cage's phone number;
Cage's belief that one should hear music as sound.
When Cage died
Cage came up to me afterwards and said,
"Striking non-intentionally at the Oriental moon",
whatever the hell that means.
I wrote this piece for John Cage;
it has something to do with John Cage.

The Universal Snail

the bright cactus whirls its water
in the black cathedral of the universe
then the white centre halts
the snail holds a room of spirals

in the white water of the cathedral
the room holds the centre of the cactus
then the bright universe halts
the black snail whirls its spirals

the room holds a universe of water
then the bright snail halts
in the black centre of the spiral
the white cactus whirls its cathedral

then the black water halts
the bright universe whirls its centre
the cactus holds a room of spirals
in the white cathedral of the snail

Mancando

variations on a lost poem

1.

you are like a window
that looks out on the image of
a city in mid-summer;

flung wide, you release a flood
of music into the still air,
scaring a clutch of sparrows
from the rooftop opposite:

the sunlight glares and warps
in your angled glass

2.

The music that you play
has opened many windows in me;
I am, in fact, a city
of open windows, windows
in the sunlight, through which
thousands of tiny birds fly
in and out, constantly.

3.

Winter: thin sunlight,
starved birds
clutching naked branches

You've walked miles
from the city's limit
just to look through
a frozen puddle's window
at a square foot
of compacted muck

Nothing coheres to these things
but a crabbed, fidgety music

4.

a window where the clouds go
lazily past the sun is not you.

you are not the symphony
of radios and car alarms
erupting from baked streets to drift
across the August rooftops,
nor the city that, one moment, halts
its jackhammer heartbeat to listen in.

you are not the blackbirds straggled
along the telegraph wire. you are
none of these things I have found.

5.

Rorschachian bird flocks
Newtonian sunlight
Euclidian windows
Mandelbrotian cities
Schoenbergian music
adjectival you

6.

One year, we watched starlings
feeding in the last of the sunlight
above the cliffs, the city behind us.

You'd left the car window rolled down,
and the radio jittered its music.

7.

The city's been razed: rubble
heaped in the squares, crows
banqueting on the unburied dead.

Even the sunlight
feels like an enemy, picking your shadow
bone-clean and crosshair-visible.

At such times, the rumble
of tank tracks snailing through the streets
beneath your boarded window
seems a kind of music.

8.

So then my master turned to me and said:
"Down below, you'll spy a walled-off city
of smoke-blackened turrets vomiting flames,
whose denizens gyre about its centre,
blind and bawling as newborns. Think of a bird
who, in error, flies through an open window
into a darkened room; how he'll panic
and tear around in circles, clamouring
to return to the light and lilt his songbook:
such is the torment of these whirligig shades."

9.

I saw you, sitting at the counter,
through the diner's grimy window,
the jukebox spinning disc after disc:
Elvis, from the Sun sessions, then
a blast of Charlie Parker's horn
blowing out the doors and clear
across the city like a gust of spring.

Joseph Stella's Reality Frenzy

Skyscrapers blindly menace the sea. Stella studies Oriental writing: dream poems, and prose that shows love's carnal paint. Exactly. Manhattan painted as a Futurist reality: speed machines, violence machines, machines that force the eye to see. Humans as metaphors for energy. Mere metaphors. Irrelevant. Exactly. Towers of light, towers of bodies, towers of dream and frenzy and pleasure and towers of poems and towers and walls and towers. And and and and and and. And the sea is a writing machine. Not a rush of monstrous lines. But the beams moved a little closer. Knife-like. Brilliant. Exactly. A writing machine. Stella shows delight in the monstrous rush of crowds, the Coney Island Chimera. Beginning to see the light. Manhattan's monstrous like the machine's dream of love. Like reality's battle for sense. Like the machine's battle with reality. Like machine and reality in nightmare love. But metaphors of what? And which was he? These are enough. Hidden. Unheard of. Exactly. These are not enough. The brilliant sea pre-figuring poems that rush and force and dream and menace and delight. Be afraid. Stella dreams of the city, the Oriental frenzy of Manhattan. Monstrous paint, dangerous paint, but not the full reality. He painted with speed and violence. Style not sense. The eye shows the painter the machine of reality. Style not delight. Speed and energy. Energy not sense. Skyscrapers full of eyes and metaphors for battle. Closer. Closer. Enough. Stella's beginning to see the city. Crowds. Streets. Lights. Violence. The monstrous reality of a Futurist Shakespeare pre-figuring the painted lines. New York, New York! Exactly. The city's a poverty machine, a pleasure machine. Painted beams and miles and miles of eyes. Crowds in a frenzy of carnal awe. A nightmare that Stella could not dream of. But he painted it. And the miners were alarmed at the knife-like reality of the paint, and the machines were mere humans, and Shakespeare was irrelevant, a mere machine, and writing was irrelevant, and studies of light were irrelevant, they were not painted, not by Stella. And poems were beginning to be like skyscrapers. Stella's metaphors were towers of light. A dream of light. A frenzy. Exactly. Exactly. Enough.

La Città Nuova: 2 constructions for Antonio Sant' Elia
"every generation will have to build its own city"

I

Patches of white rain frame the rickety day. The alphabet is a stretched, shadowy structure. A film's cracked conclusion: steely heaps of blue brick.

White patches on the film: blue rain steels into the rickety brick. Cracked shadows stretch & frame the heaped day's structures in alphabetical conclusions.

A shadow alphabet rains onto the blue structures. Patched film, its stretched & rickety steel frames. The day is white, cracked, concluding in heaps of brick.

Blue steel & white brick are heaped conclusively in the film's shadowy frames. The alphabet's structures are rickety. Stretched rain is patched into the day's cracks.

Frames of film shadow the alphabet. The rainy day is heaped in patches of stretched steel & rickety conclusions. White structure, blue cracks in the brick.

Shadows patch an alphabet on the stretched white day. The rickety structure concludes in a frame of blue steel, heaps of cracked brick filmed with rain.

II

the fire escapes clatter up the walls
repetitious inky arpeggios
everything is happening &
all at once hissing yellow
repetitious inky arpeggios
jasmine tongues the gas jets
all at once hissing yellow
igniting the interstices of
jasmine tongues the gas jets
everything is arpeggios
igniting the interstices of
repetitious inky gas jets
everything is arpeggios
jasmine tongues the walls
repetitious inky gas jets
igniting the inky arpeggios
jasmine tongues the walls
fire tongues the gas jets
igniting the inky arpeggios
everything is hissing yellow
fire tongues the gas jets
everything is happening &
everything is hissing yellow
the fire escapes, clatters up the walls

The Scaffold

of brawny blue
girders erected
beside a disused
building shedding
bricks & green
paint-flecks with
1 crane hulked
behind it I
planned to use as
a simile for
purple toadflax
in a poem named
'Purple Toadflax'
but which in
redraft after
redraft after
redraft was erased
altogether now
supports nothing
but a blank
wall, a white
immensity

III

Brummagem

"Most of it has never been seen."
—Roy Fisher, *City*

I have no real use for maps. I tend to come to an understanding of the city through the memorisation of landmarks, the knowledge of the senses, and of the feet. To think of the city as an abstract totality—an **A-Z**, or a **Rough Guide To**...—is to reduce it utterly. The city must be discovered inch by inch with the aid of the body, as one discovers a lover.

Who has, in truth, seen the city? Eliot withdrew in disgust; Pound plunged his head in sand and dreamt of Doric columns. So far the city has not been given its due praise: it elicits as much terror and revolt in the poetic observer as it does awe, or love, or respect. Maybe those other voices could not reconcile the city's disorder, its violence and destructive exuberance, to their schemata, their vision of a divinely ordained harmony. Ideally, the city poet will not be constrained by such notions as 'beauty', or 'perfection'. Rather, she will go out amongst the rubble, the smokestacks, marching to the rhythms of faulty car alarms and heavy machinery grinding in distant factories, her eye a permanently shuttering camera lens, her body a mindless concatenation of sensory data.

The most appropriate visual analogy I can suggest for the city's immensity of sprawl is the reproduction of bacteria observed through a microscope, spoolings and unspoolings, clouds accumulating in time-lapse. There is, certainly, a pattern to both the metropolitan and bacterial cultures, but it cannot be discerned or decoded, neither in part, nor in totality.

Cities of the mind: a system of mental visualisation, whereby an imaginary city is fabricated, brick by brick, avenue by avenue, each element of which is designed to correspond to a specific memory belonging to the 'architect'. So, for example, the fragments of Shakespeare that the architect has retained over the course of her life might be signified by a sparsely occupied multi-storey carpark, fizzing with fluorescents; whilst the smashed glass of a vandalised phone booth might stand in for a repressed memory of childhood abuse. The real city differs insofar as its referents refer back only to themselves.

Silence will not come out of silence, and if transcendence is ever to be found, it will be in the city. Imagine: standing on an overpass at rush hour, watching late light flare blue then gold then deep amber in the windows of towerblocks; or in a crowded bar, when all conversation stops at once, and a beautiful woman happens to laugh. These things are of more worth than any lucid moment experienced on a mountain peak, or alone among malting pines, because they are incongruous, because they are earned: as when, standing in the backyard, exhaling shot-glassfuls of steam, you wait for the moon to reveal itself from behind a scurl of cloud—full and cream as a reptile's egg, a Guinness crown.

Through a coffeeshop window, I watched a man explain the central tenets of liberal humanism in mime to a girl selling *The Big Issue*. First, he made a Nazi salute, and frowned and shook his head whilst doing so; and his counter-argument took the form of a jovial wave of his hand, a smile and a nod. The girl looked bemused, but his point seemed clear to me. A light spring rain was falling on Victoria Square, and made a sound like the earth sighing.

The truest poetic response to the city, the form which would most authentically reflect its monstrosity, its formless perfection, would be, essentially, a list of everything—every thought, every sensation, every rapid disjunction of consciousness —experienced by every human and animal occupant who had ever resided within the city's boundaries. This is, of course, impossible.

There are no words commensurate to those mutant appurtenances (a phone-booth with all its glass ruptured and pooled at its base; crippled umbrellas and broke-backed books sprawled on public benches acned with overnight rain; empty garage forecourts, concrete tumours marking where the pumps have been removed) that assault the eye's ease as we move about the city. The streets are rowdy with them, and they shape our consciousness more than we would care to think, yet no-one has given a name to these shattered ghosts, exiles from some republic of the broken, the botched. Some mornings, it is easier to feel kinship for a **HAZARDOUS MATERIALS** sign hanging from a rusted chain-link fence than for one's own neighbour.

"Most of it has never been seen". A clarification: The city has been seen a great deal, and been condemned every time. Louis MacNeice, for one, conceived of a mechanised Hell in the grind and swelter of the production line, and feared for the deleterious effects such conditions would have upon the minds, bodies and souls of the labouring classes. He was right, perhaps, but the city offers consolations even now: the women's hospital with its antiseptic mask of ivy; light at rush hour scaling a Chinese pagoda tile by ridged tile; frontages on New Street glazed with bulbous plastic sheeting; monstrous cranes and towerblocks broaching the jaundiced sky like impertinent questions. Either MacNeice did not see their equivalent in his day, or he chose not to comment.

IV

Municipal Amenities

Swifts

1 what I say

Fraught June & the swifts feed
in clay-baked air over Marlborough Street,
nifty shadows pocking from kerb
to kerb across hotplate blacktop

Apostrophes & ampersands,
their flicking & sniping
through tough light brags bad grammar

Lacking patience for the sentence,
its measured pace, its clarity,
they score doodled garbles
on the skied white, body their whipped brisks
through poplarish highs & pining dwarfs
to leaf their shivered greens
with a flown & flying go

2 *what they say*

                                 flying brags

                  bad brisks

clarity: measured clarity   the tough body

               the sentence, it's over

flicking clay-baked shadows   the kerb garbles

              blacktop white in June

                      light, pining
                      lacking
    poplarish apostrophes   sniping
                      flicking
            a   pocking, flown
               nifty

    doodled ampersands   &   leaf

                  &   whipped

        &   across

  &   the
      &
          street
    feed   go

             swifts , flying
     a shivered
grammar

26/06/05

A neighbour's tree
clenches inside
its big green
fist one shrivelled
branch that droops,
weighted with crunchy
light-brown leaves,
catching & having
caught, needing to be
lopped, my thoughts
since May, it now
June, a Sunday, cool
& still & nothing
doing: coffee, treacle-
thick & strong, the radio
on (choral songs) & stacked
dishes drying in blue
noon light, writing
with no clear purpose
other than to stop
this crisp day
from shrivelling or
ending just yet

First Comes Being
for Jon

1

The overhead train
is a thunderous concern

Summer's a racket of sunlight
& of shock-blossom

The hotplate paving odours
like a woman, the shimmer

BEWARE OF CYCLES

I find your scrawl in the underpass
chalk dust & silvered leaves

I have passed through estates
of a similar salmon

& stumble-slumbered under blue of bloom
{*gentianella campestris*}

2

"Hot rain on the veranda,
 Theodore." Read that over:
"Hot rain on the veranda,
 Theodore." Read that over:
"Hot rain on the veranda,
 Theodore & the screen door
 has shut us out in it."

§

A tigerish light tussles & rolls
on molten tarmac;
fools hold books of sand
that hiss & spit
a dog-tongued heat-struck alphabet—
"Viva! Viva! Alpha! Omega!"—
whilst lawnmowers whirr
their steel teeth somewhere
west of Hiroshima:
wheesht wheesht wheesht.

Sundials bisected
with their own scalpel-sharp shadows;
weeds unfurling under
the raw feral sun:
as words press down
on these isolate units
of reality, so feet will press
the pith from fruit
for the sweet wine—poetry.

§

the sun licks at the trees
hot vishnu skies
nature's children undress

"right then straight on"
dust hushes through the streets:
shuttered shops & concrete tetrahedrons
roll on for miles

later, a ruby moon balloons
from Brum's estates: a lustrous lunar flame
tumbles onto burned-out motors
& muddled flats

§

Satellites glister in space,
silent bells:
NASA listens in—
ping   *ping*   *ping*
      ping   *ping*
              ping
                              ping   *ping*   *ping*

3

& of the train
       of bloom like a racket
              of salmon

the overhead
       is a shimmer
             & a silvered underpass

{beware leaves of a similar chalk}

paving cycles through
       estates: odours of concern: I have
             passed under a sunlight

blue woman,
       the thunderous summer's
             shock-blossom

I find your *gentianella campestris*
       & stumble-slumbered
             scrawl in the hotplate dust

The Magic Hour

& when leaves are blown back in an upsurging breeze with accompaniment
of music as of leaves blowing back in an upsurging breeze
or some near approximation of &c, say the rustle of a dead man's
acquisitions, a life bartered & boxed in a Maybaked parking garage,
all his prized possessions, the Sunday china, bronze boxing trophies &c
wrapped in sepia headlines, the baby photos under anaesthetic tissue
& the joggers, long as anything & the sunbathers thinking of anything
but melanoma, thinking *Platypi or -pusses?* thinking *I must get these shoes*
& the typewriter clucks & pigeon-puffs its speckled paper scroll,
a nation of etch & of scent & of sprawl & of the associations of &c,
the writer at his window examining a sunstricken leaf, a nation &c,
because there are no words but *splutter*, because there are no &c
& Godard's Champs Elysée, tin-tinted leaves martially aligned upon the trees
& a Kurasawa snowdrift, & Eisenstein's uprising lions, saluting atop their &c,
& Manhattan, jazz-pulsating, is a neon detonation of girders & of hotfooting
          taxicabs,
yeah, & Venice wears a red hood & shimmies in her undies underwater,
& Frisco's vertiginous with the clanging of trams, plish of gulls in the clashed
          froth
rimming Alcatraz, & I think I missed out Barcelona, her tangerine *excuse-mes*
& to catch that moment, that godgifted sprung luminescence & the shadows
all of an aqueous artery-throb in the coffee-dunked late afternoon sunlight,
          yes,
& throatmurmur also of the collar-dove & of the coot & of the &c—sounds
so real they do not register as &c & merely add to an uncanny sense of &c—&
those exact birds looping the thermals & airways re-enacted in fractions
in the shot-glass frontages of towerblocks & boys with their arms outstretched

"The confused streams aligned"

Scrawled wedges of colour
aspire towards clarity—
the sky's clipped blue,
buildings bleared
behind midday's
haze of pollutants
like a blackboard's
chalk-dust ghosts, the gospel
tabernacle's gold & navy
Your first birthday
was spoiled sign,
ripped fistfuls of blossom
that whirr & collide
with the Wheatsheaf yardies—
sifted husks of an afternoon,
chance assembly
of objects beneath the sun
then to glister & be
components of some April,
some emblematic spring

"My Best Balloon"

i

The scraps of its colours
oppose and are Xeroxed
by the landscape it rose from—
the sky the clean blue
of a Titian; the washcloth
snagged on a nail
in the neighbour's yard,
grubby turquoise; burgundy
and clashed gold of spring trees—
each component conspiring
to reduce the balloon to
a cipher of their precise
unanimity in air

ii

The sun's prism
snared in cloud then
fractured into shards
of yellow, crimson &
greenish blue is

the wavering mirror
of the hot-air balloon
whose bud of flame
we see flare split-
seconds before its roar

can be heard here beside
the canal at the end
of a crisp painterly day
of which this balloon
is the ascendant ghost

The Gingko Tree in August

These fanned leaves smattering
    in an upstart municipal wind
amongst splayed stripling branches
    are contingencies of light, glittered
flakes raggedly contorting,
    displaying silver undersides
to the discriminate eye. Such
    commotion upwards and out
as energises its fluid extremities
    devolves from the transfixed
hub, a hungry trunk skirted
    by iron railings and rooted
in white concrete which repeats
    in variations to comprise
the city entire, of which the gingko's
    flickered leaves are embryo
and emblem. Each one concludes
    in a permeable edge—

A Congregation

torn branches scattered
round the base
of the hawthorn,
crisped leaves
fiercely clinging
to the jumbled wood,
are kindling only
to the raked blaze
of their being
gathered today
beneath this tree
whose lobed leaves
remain delicately
beaded after shock
August torrents—

Prune

lop back
to skyward
   'now'
of trunk

Municipal Amenities

for Rochelle

1.

make a poem which begins:
you said the music was
"more like trees than buildings"
which i liked & used to
make a poem which begins:
you said the music was
"more like trees than buildings"
which i liked & used to
make a poem which begins:
you said the music was
"more like trees than buildings"
which i liked & used to
make a poem which begins

2.

plum tree, pear tree,
sheen-leafed eucalyptus
& sycamore blether
out of the shared fug
of namelessness then
cohere in the shagged fur
of a city evening this july

3.

a milk float
a flat ukulele
an eaten lake
a neat flute
a fault-line
a little meat
a fake tune
o make me mute

4.

tram	washed	rain	quick	new	fresh		fresh	new	quick	rain	washed	tram
tram		tramlines			lines		lines		linestram			tram
washed		washedwith			with		with		withwashed			washed
rain		rainwater:			water		water		waterrain			rain
quick		quicksilver			silver		silver		silverquick			quick
new		newwords			words		words		wordsnew			new
fresh		freshforged			forged		forged		forgedfresh			fresh
lines with	water silver	words forged					forged words	silver water	with lines			

lines with	water silver	words forged					forged words	silver water	with lines			
fresh		freshforged			forged		forged		forgedfresh			fresh
new		newwords			words		words		wordsnew			new
quick		quicksilver			silver		silver		silverquick			quick
rain		rainwater:			water		water		waterrain			rain
washed		washedwith			with		with		withwashed			washed
tram		tramlines			lines		lines		linestram			tram
tram	washed	rain quick	new fresh				fresh new	quick rain	washed tram			

5.

On the eleventh, smoke coiled up
from the warehouses tucked
behind the railway tracks
& smudged July's bright blue
with a pillar, taller & blacker
than the backyard poplar,
snagged with scorched scraps
that rode its thermals & looped
through baked fuzzy air
like birds at dusk rising & feeding

Earlier, a "suspect package" had closed
the city down & I'd walked home
along the canal, stilled black water
ablaze with eely slivers of light
to the right of me, viral
& profane bursts of wild flowers
to my left & everything
had seemed broken & appropriate
as a battered fence throttled
with ivy that's shrivelled to tough gold
through the parched, stretched summer

6.

you liked the lines *bats*
unclip themselves from the dark
like so many neckties
which i wrote some time ago
& couldnt find a home for so
i've decided to make a gift
of them for you here:
                    bats
unclip themselves from the dark
like so many neckties

7.

a jaunty breeze today shook
bunches of orange berries
suspended among the drooped
green tresses of a tree
that grows behind the schoolyard's
low concrete wall; a reminder
to later ask you its name

Joinery / Refurbishments
for George

stars are plunder & snipped
into chain-link, stare
there, clamped in gaps, ware-
houses, hypermarkets
the blocked grids straining

I take these, enough, & you
some other thing, that
bank-side tree stripped but
for some half-dozen red
apples round unexpected

what a scrawny tree we ask
to carry so much, I mean
they looked heavy, the
apples, the red apples looked
quite heavy is what I meant

16/08/2005

The moon you said looked
"like an apricot" was obscured
when I went to see if I
could see from my backyard

Undersides of thin clouds
mustered above the roof
caught some of its light

& so did the poplar's
highest branches:
such a hulked black net

to snag the delicate after-
image of an unseen apricot
moon in August

Summer

On alternate days an unabashed lapis all across the city
like today a pressed & laundered summer shirt of a day
yes with the tree stump's ruffled shelves of orange fungus
all glossed in the bold blue luminous just for a moment
but later on come back to check the hangup socks not yet
dry & the sunlight's moved on behind the monster poplar
50 foot to its crest is my best reckoning you can see it
or could from a wooden bench in the small playground
across the street from the house & the fungus doesn't
shine anymore just desiccated ivy crowding round
a window just mint ice cream bars & a good strong
coffee or several over the course of a day coarse black
residue crusting at the bottom of the mug & so what
does Doctor Bill Williams say he says *Summer!*
                                    the painting is organised

26/8/06

Ah, the Gillian Welch record's
just finished, leaving the sound
of Rochelle sanding the table with
3 different gradations of paper,
but that last melody's lingering,
a song of bluebirds & of winter.

    Outside,
a slate sky threatening rain,
the poplar leaves flitting silver
in a jagged intermittent wind,
occasional birds—a wren, a crow,
earlier a sudden clutter of pigeons—
stuttering overhead. This is home.
The shavings accumulate. It
is finished. "Can I feel the top?"
"Yes." Smooth sheen, rough
at the edges—

The Ginsberg Address

Look here now dammit Allen if I ever said I didnt appreciate
    your poetry
that was plainly bullshit because I read your poem 'In back of
    the real' Allen
this morning in the front room Allen after a cup of coffee in fine
    weather
such clarity such rickety music so that later I saw something I
    often see Allen
similar to what you describe so clearly Allen both in that poem
    & in others of yours
on the approach to the city when the train slows & the battered
    landscape Allen
stage by stage emerges in pieces Allen from the roar of its
    rushing past the windows
thats called 'Relativity' I think for example an alphabet of cranes
    necking up Allen
from the citys wreckage big weed bushes Allen all along the
    rusted train tracks
blue dusk heaped with clouds a rosy light drooling down
    among the warehouses Allen
gulls washing at rain pooled in gravel ditches Allen that darkly
    mirror the sky
then startled into flight by the passing train their wings
    shivering the surface Allen
you know what Im talking about Allen everything clean &
    shocked like when a photo
Allen because of your poem Allen because of your poem Allen
    because of your poem

On Condition That

If only the night were not so jittery with sodium
If only there were traffic on the A road,
the shudder of hulking concrete struts
If only the Absolute Mystery would show itself fully, just once,
& not as "fractured light", because it's always "fractured light",
& not as fuzztoned smoke around a half-moon
If only I had written "in Beverly Hills, the jacaranda trees
are beginning to bloom", & not Raymond Chandler
If only I were Raymond Chandler
If only this city did not rattle & clang & beset me with neon
from every yammering storefront & tattoo parlour window
like some monstropolous jukebox blaring the opening bars
of 'Spoilt Victorian Child' by the Fall over & over & over
If only I had composed those lines earlier in my career,
I would not find them so embarrassing now
If only I could be said to have a career
If only this city *were* in fact a monstropolous jukebox,
& I had a jivetalking fingerpopping pocketful of change to pump
        into its slot
If only I did not waste so much time listening to Karate
at high volume, in low light, kicking the air,
then something at least would get written, even if it was only
'angled black glass snags the winter sun:
a haggard baseball in a pitcher's glove'
If only more songs contained the word 'dirigibles'
If only our shared language amounted to more than
Clearance Sale : *Bifidus Digestivum* : **Emergency Stop**

NOTES

'Storm Journal: *26th July 2006*': Nikos Kazantzakis, in *Report to Greco* (1961), notes: "Genghis Khan wore an iron ring with two words engraved upon it: *Rastì Roustì*—'Might is Right'." (London: Faber, 1973: p 330).

'Bat-watching : summer : second night': Both quotations are from Alan Watts' essay 'Beat Zen, Square Zen and Zen', originally published in the *Chicago Review* in 1958, and reprinted in *The Portable Beat Reader*, edited by Ann Charters (New York: Viking Penguin, 1992).

'Thirteen': This poem consists of anagrams, or semi-anagrams, of every line in Wallace Stevens' 'Thirteen Ways of Looking at a Blackbird'.

'Autumn Processional' was created by repeatedly mutating an untitled poem of mine through online translation software, and cherry-picking the best results. Below is the original. Unfortunately, I felt it was too similar to a section of *The Descent of Winter* by William Carlos Williams to warrant inclusion on its own merits:

> a tilt in the weather September
> halfway gone leaves crisping or
> hurled in gusts light of a clarity
> which is clearly not the summer's
>
> Sparkbrook & the school roof ripped
> being rebuilt shredded tarpaulin
> flickering on the new black benches
> pits in the concrete lopsided cones
>
> certain trees already mere stripped
> branches bracing crystal blue just
> a last few trembling yellow leaves just
> a few thin cloud patches here & there

'Dada Jukebox': Phrases in this poem originate from any number of sources, including cut-ups and mutations of my own making, unwanted spam emails, Donald Barthelme's short stories, Terry Riley's record sleeves, Tristan Tzara's Dada manifestoes, and a whiteboard in room 107 of Warwick University's humanities building. Some of the phrases, meanwhile, originate from none of these places.

'To Be Bewildered': This poem, a tribute to the composer John Cage, is an assemblage of phrases from *American Originals: Interviews with 25 Contemporary Composers*, edited by Geoff Smith and Nicola Walker Smith (London: Faber, 1994).

'Joseph Stella's Reality Frenzy': A permutational cutup of a paragraph dealing with the American Futurist painter on page 174 of Michael Pye's *Maximum City* (London: Picador, 1993).

'The Scaffold': The scaffold in question is no longer standing.

'Brummagem': Perhaps taking Bloom's anxiety of influence a little to heart, I avoided reading Roy Fisher for a long time, worried that, as a fellow Midlands-based writer, he would come to dominate my own style once I had. I was right.

"The confused streams aligned": The title is a quotation from William Carlos Williams' poem 'Paterson: the Falls'.

"My Best Balloon": The title is taken from Donald Barthelme's story 'The Great Hug', from *Sixty Stories* (London: Penguin, 1993).

'Summer': The phrase *'Summer! / The painting is organised'* is a quotation from Williams' poem 'The Corn Harvest', from the doctor's final collection *Pictures from Brueghel*, which can be found in volume II of the *Collected Poems* (Manchester: Carcanet, 2000).

'26/8/06': The Gillian Welch record in question was *Hell Among the Yearlings* (Acony Records, 1998), and the song was 'Winter's Come and Gone'.

'On Condition That': The Raymond Chandler quotation is from his 1949 novel *The Little Sister*, included in *The Lady in the Lake and Other Novels* (London: Penguin, 2001).